09/05

$19.95

TOP TEN COUNTRIES OF RECENT IMMIGRANTS

THE PHILIPPINES

A MyReportLinks.com Book

SUZANNE LIEURANCE

MyReportLinks.com Books

an imprint of

 Enslow Publishers, Inc. **E**

Box 398, 40 Industrial Road
Berkeley Heights, NJ 07922
USA

MyReportLinks.com Books, an imprint of Enslow Publishers, Inc. MyReportLinks®
is a registered trademark of Enslow Publishers, Inc.

Library of Congress Cataloging-in-Publication Data

Lieurance, Suzanne.
  The Philippines / Suzanne Lieurance.
     v. cm. — (Top ten countries of recent immigrants)
Includes bibliographical references and index.
Contents: The pearl of the Orient — Land and climate — Culture —
Economy — History — Filipino Americans today.
  ISBN 0-7660-5175-7
  1. Philippines—Juvenile literature. 2. Filipino Americans—Juvenile
literature. [1. Philippines. 2. Filipino Americans.] I. Title. II.
Series.
  DS655.L48 2004
  959.9—dc22
                                    2003015241

Printed in the United States of America

10 9 8 7 6 5 4 3 2 1

To Our Readers:
Through the purchase of this book, you and your library gain access to the Report Links that specifically back up this book.
The Publisher will provide access to the Report Links that back up this book and will keep these Report Links up to date on **www.myreportlinks.com** for three years from the book's first publication date.
We have done our best to make sure all Internet addresses in this book were active and appropriate when we went to press. However, the author and the Publisher have no control over, and assume no liability for, the material available on those Internet sites or on other Web sites they may link to.
The usage of the MyReportLinks.com Books Web site is subject to the terms and conditions stated on the Usage Policy Statement on **www.myreportlinks.com**.
A password may be required to access the Report Links that back up this book. The password is found on the bottom of page 4 of this book.
Any comments or suggestions can be sent by e-mail to comments@myreportlinks.com or to the address on the back cover.

Photo Credits: © Corel Corporation, pp. 1, 9 (flags), 11, 22 ; AP/Wide World Photos, p. 39; Artville, p. 3; Defense Visual Information Center/National Archives and Records Administration, p. 33; Enslow Publishers, Inc., p. 17; Library of Congress, pp. 24, 30, 34, 36; LIKHA, 43; MyReportLinks.com Books, pp. 4, back cover; Philippines Department of Tourism, p. 26; Pista sa Nayon, p. 45; The Mariners' Museum, p. 28; The Philippine Tarsier Foundation, Inc., p. 19; UNESCO, p. 12; United States Geological Survey, p. 14.

Cover Photo: Rice terraces, flags, © Corel Corporation; Filipino girl and boy, Photos.com.

Contents

959.9
LIE
2004

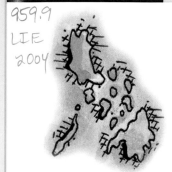

THE PHILIPPINES

Report Links **4**

The Philippines Facts **9**

1 The Pearl of the Orient Seas **10**

2 Land and Climate **16**

3 Culture **21**

4 Economy **27**

5 History **31**

6 Filipino Americans Today **40**

Chapter Notes **46**

Further Reading **47**

Index **48**

About MyReportLinks.com Books

MyReportLinks.com Books
Great Books, Great Links, Great for Research!

The Report Links listed on the following four pages can save you hours of research time by **instantly** bringing you to the best Web sites relating to your report topic.

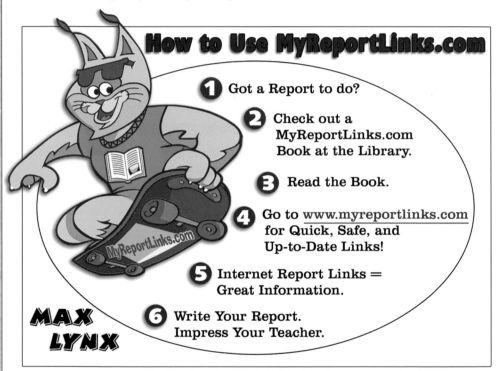

How to Use MyReportLinks.com

1 Got a Report to do?

2 Check out a MyReportLinks.com Book at the Library.

3 Read the Book.

4 Go to www.myreportlinks.com for Quick, Safe, and Up-to-Date Links!

5 Internet Report Links = Great Information.

6 Write Your Report. Impress Your Teacher.

MAX LYNX

The pre-evaluated Web sites are your links to source documents, photographs, illustrations, and maps. They also provide links to dozens—even hundreds—of Web sites about your report subject.

MyReportLinks.com Books and the MyReportLinks.com Web site save you time and make report writing easier than ever!

Please see "To Our Readers" on the copyright page for important information about this book, the MyReportLinks.com Web site, and the Report Links that back up this book. Please enter **ITP5345** if asked for a password.

Report Links

The Internet sites described below can be accessed at
http://www.myreportlinks.com

▶**Philippines—A Country Study**   *EDITOR'S CHOICE

This Library of Congress site is a comprehensive look at the
Philippines. Information about Philippine geography, culture, history,
government, economics, religion, language, and other subjects can be
found here.

▶**The *World Factbook*: Philippines**   *EDITOR'S CHOICE

This page from the CIA *World Factbook* contains an overview of
the Philippines. Statistics having to do with the country's geography,
people, government, economy, communications, transportation, and
military are covered here.

▶**Wow Philippines**   *EDITOR'S CHOICE

This is the official site of the Philippines Department of Tourism.
Here you will find maps, useful Filipino phrases, local customs,
tourist information, and other resources for planning a visit to
the Philippines.

▶**The Official Government Portal of the Republic**   *EDITOR'S CHOICE
of the Philippines

This official government site of the Philippines presents information
about the country's agriculture, economy, education, transportation, and
more. A biography of President Gloria Macapagal-Arroyo is included.

▶**The World of 1898: The Spanish-American War**   *EDITOR'S CHOICE

The Spanish-American War resulted in the United States controlling
the Philippines. This Library of Congress presentation contains
photographs, maps, documents, chronologies, and personal accounts
of the war.

▶**The Philippine Centennial Celebration**   *EDITOR'S CHOICE

In 1998 the Philippines celebrated its centennial as an independent
nation. This site commemorates the Philippine Revolution and
first hundred years of the Republic of the Philippines in articles,
documents, biographies, and more.

Report Links

The Internet sites described below can be accessed at http://www.myreportlinks.com

▶**BBC News: Joseph Estrada**

Joseph Estrada was a famous Filipino movie star before becoming president of the Philippines. A military-backed uprising forced him to abandon the office in 2001. His trials for a variety of corruption charges continue to this day.

▶**BBC News: The Earth's Ring of Fire**

The Ring of Fire is a ring-shaped area in the Pacific Ocean where earthquakes and volcanoes are common. The Philippines is the deadliest point in the ring. This article discusses the physics behind the Ring of Fire.

▶***Bubalus mindorensis:* Tamaraw**

The tamaraw, native to the island of Mindoro, is a critically endangered small buffalo. This site covers tamaraw characteristics, taxonomy, reproduction, ecology, behavior, conservation status, and more.

▶**Dancing Anew on the Stairways to Heaven**

The Banaue rice terraces, sometimes referred to as the eighth wonder of the world, are on the Philippine island of Luzon. Here you will learn more about the terraces, their history, and the people who built them.

▶**Ferdinand Magellan**

This site offers a biography of Ferdinand Magellan, the first European explorer to sail across the Pacific and the first to set foot on the Philippines.

▶**Ferdinand E. Marcos**

Ferdinand Marcos, the president of the Philippines for more than twenty years, was finally forced into exile when mass protests demanded he step down. Here you will find a brief overview of his life and political career.

▶**Fire and Mud—Mount Pinatubo**

This site contains the complete text of a book about the eruption of Mount Pinatubo in June of 1991 and tells about the effects it has had on the global climate.

▶**Gloria Macapagal-Arroyo**

Gloria Macapagal-Arroyo was sworn in as the Philippines' fourteenth president in 2001. Here you will find her biography as well as a list of her accomplishments, activities, initiatives, speeches, photographs, and more.

Report Links

The Internet sites described below can be accessed at http://www.myreportlinks.com

▶**José Rizal**

This site is dedicated to José Rizal, the official national hero of the Philippines. Learn about a true renaissance figure, who was a writer, artist, philosopher, physician, scientist, educator, musician, and Filipino nationalist leader.

▶**The LIKHA Pilipino Folk Ensemble**

The LIKHA Pilipino Folk Ensemble, based in the San Francisco Bay Area, preserves and presents Philippine culture in dance, literature, crafts, music, and art. This site offers a history of the group as well as a list of its upcoming performances.

▶**Lopez Memorial Museum: Fernando C. Amorsolo**

Fernando Amorsolo was the first Filipino artist to earn the Philippines' National Artist award. Here you can learn about the painter and see some of his work.

▶**Lopez Memorial Museum: Juan Luna**

Juan Luna was a Filipino realist painter who received global acclaim. This site provides information about his life and work and offers a virtual tour of his paintings.

▶**Manuel L. Quezon (1878–1944)**

In 1935, Manuel Quezon became the first elected leader of the Philippines. Here you will learn about his life and his relationship with General Douglas MacArthur.

▶**Mount Apo**

Mount Apo is the tallest peak in the Philippines. Here you will learn about this extinct volcano, its social and environmental importance, and its vegetation.

▶**National Statistics Office, Republic of the Philippines**

The Philippines National Statistics Office (NSO) collects and compiles statistics about the Philippines. Here you will find the most current statistics on population, literacy, unemployment, inflation, trade, and agriculture.

▶**Northern Luzon, Philippines**

In this article from RiceWorld.org, you can read about the legendary rice terraces of Luzon, Philippines. Photos of the terraces are also included.

Report Links

The Internet sites described below can be accessed at http://www.myreportlinks.com

▶ **Perry-Castañeda Library Map Collection: Philippines Maps**

You can view current and historic maps of the Philippine islands on this site from the Perry-Castañeda Library Map Collection

▶ **The Philippine Tarsier Foundation**

The tiny Philippine tarsier is found nowhere else on earth but several islands of the Philippines. Learn about efforts to save this species.

▶ **Philippines—Islands Under Siege, June 2003**

This PBS site chronicles the ongoing war between Muslim separatists and the Philippine government. It also presents a time line of conflict within the Philippines, starting with the United States occupation after the Spanish-American War.

▶ **Pista Congratulates our Pulitzer Prize Winners**

Byron Acohido and Alex Tizon each won Pulitzer Prizes in journalism in 1997. Both journalists are Filipino Americans who write for the *Seattle Times*. Here you will find an article about their achievements.

▶ **Tectonics and Volcanoes of the Philippines**

The volcanoes of the Philippines are the most deadly and costly in the world. This site from the University of North Dakota's Volcano World is dedicated to studying volcanic activity in the Philippines.

▶ ***Time* 100: Corazon Aquino**

Corazon Aquino was elected president of the Philippines after Ferdinand Marcos was forced from power in the People Power Revolution of 1986. Here you will find an article about Aquino's life and accomplishments.

▶ **Villa, Pancho**

Not to be confused with the Mexican revolutionary of the same name, the Filipino Pancho Villa was one of the most famous boxers of the 1920s. This site offers a brief biography of the flyweight champion.

▶ **Welcome to the History of the Philippines: Pearl of the Orient Seas**

This site contains an in-depth history of the Philippines from 40,000 B.C. to A.D. 1998, with articles about the Spanish and American colonial periods, the Spanish-American War, the Katipunan Rebellion, and more.

The Philippines Facts

▶ Official Name

Republika ng Pilipinas (Republic of the Philippines)[1]

▶ Capital

Manila

▶ Population

84,525,639 (2002 est.)[2]

▶ Land Area

115,830 square miles (300,000 square kilometers)

▶ Highest Point

Mount Apo 9,692 ft (2,954 m)

▶ Largest Cities

Manila, Da Vao, Cebu, Quezon City

▶ Monetary Unit

Philippine peso (which is divided into 100 centavos)

▶ Type of Government

Republic

▶ Location

Southeastern Asia, in the Pacific. The Philippines is an archipelago between the Philippine Sea and the South China Sea, east of Vietnam.

▶ Language(s) Spoken

Two official languages—Filipino or Pilipino, which is based on Tagalog, and English; eight major dialects: Tagalog, Cebuano, Ilocan, Hiligaynon or Ilonggo, Bicol, Waray, Pampango, and Pangasinense

▶ National Flower

Sampaguita

▶ National Bird

Philippine eagle

▶ National Tree

Narra tree

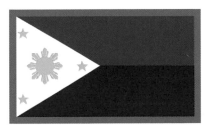

▶ Flag

Two equal horizontal bands of blue (top) and red with a white equilateral triangle based on the hoist side; in the center of the triangle is a yellow sun with eight primary rays (each containing three individual rays), and in each corner of the triangle is a small yellow five-pointed star

The Pearl of the Orient Seas

The Philippines is an archipelago, or group of islands, in southeastern Asia. The country's official name is Republic of the Philippines. Because of its beauty, it is often called "the pearl of the orient seas." The islands of the Philippines were formed millions of years ago by volcanoes. Although 7,107 islands make up this country, people live on only 2,000 of them.

The Philippines is a country of rich contrasts. Here, you will find tropical paradises with swaying palm trees on soft, white sandy beaches next to a bright blue sea. You will also find bustling cities with high-rise buildings, hotels, modern shopping malls, casinos, and restaurants. Most of the people of the Philippines do not live in the cities, however. About 70 percent of the people live in barrios, or small villages, in the provinces. They mostly rely on farming and fishing to make their living. Many people in barrios do not have running water or electricity in their homes. Most people born in the barrios usually grow up and spend their entire lives there. Their farthest travels may take them to the nearest town to buy or sell fruits and vegetables or enjoy a fiesta.[1]

▶ The Philippine People

People from the Philippines are called Filipinos. In keeping with their Asian culture, Filipinos feel they must maintain their dignity or self-respect at all times, which they call *amor proprio*.[2] In just a little more than a

▲ *Farming in some areas of the Philippines is still done the same way it has been done for centuries.*

century, the Philippine people have lived under the regimes of two large colonial powers—first, Spain, for more than three hundred years, and then the United States, for nearly fifty years. Their relationships with both countries have not been easy and have, in some cases, had tragic consequences. But the people of the Philippines have endured the years of colonial rule to form their own government, gotten rid of a president through a bloodless revolution, and have been governed by women twice in their short history as a republic.

▶ From Rice Terraces to Volcanoes

There are dramatic sights to see in the Philippines—everything from rice terraces built thousands of years ago

The Banaue rice terraces on Luzon give the province a unique landscape. It is said that the best rice grown in the Philippines is cultivated by the poorest farmers working in the highest and least accessible areas, like this one.

to inactive and active volcanoes. The heart of the country is Manila, the capital and largest city. It is also the Philippines' shipping, trade, and cultural capital. Many Filipinos from the provinces go to Manila to attend school or to find work.

The Banaue Rice Terraces are located on Luzon, an island in the northern Philippines. These rice terraces are sometimes called the eighth wonder of the world. They appear to be stairways to heaven but are really rice paddies terraced from the top to the bottom of the mountainside. These terraces have an ingenious irrigation system that channels water from the highest terraces down into the lowest ones.

Quezon City is the former capital of the Philippines. It is four times bigger than the city of Manila in area. The World Expo was held there in 2002. Many tourists looking for sandy, white beaches go to Boracay, a bone-shaped island in the Philippines. Boracay's beach was voted the best beach in the world by three Asian publications.

Mount Pinatubo is a volcano in Central Luzon. It was dormant for 450 years, but in June 1991, it erupted violently. Scientists knew that the volcano was about to explode, so about fifty-eight thousand people were evacuated from the area, many of them servicemen and their families stationed at Clark Air Force Base, which has since been closed.

Just as the volcano became most active, Typhoon Yunya hit the islands, making things even worse. The ash and lava were turned into gray and white mud, and daylight became pitch-dark night. The eruption was one of the worst in recorded history. The ash from it was a foot deep. Even with the evacuation, many people died as showers of ash and sand billowed up from Pinatubo, covering and collapsing roofs of houses and other buildings.

Famous Filipinos and Filipinas

Men and women of the Philippines have made their mark on their country and the world in many fields, including literature, art, and politics.

Maria Josefa Gabriela Silang was an Ilocano freedom fighter in the eighteenth century. After her husband, Diego, was assassinated, she took up the movement to free the Philippines from Spanish rule. She fought with great courage. On September 30, 1763, she and about one hundred other members of the revolution were executed

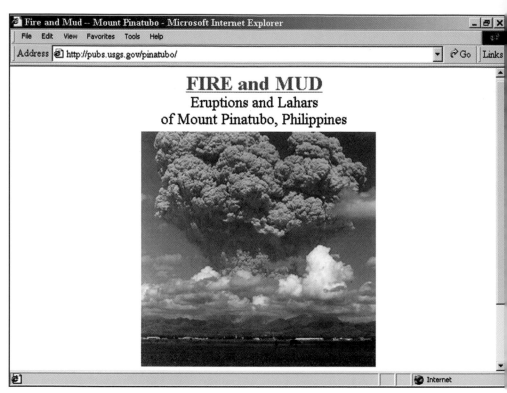

Fire and Mud -- Mount Pinatubo - Microsoft Internet Explorer

File Edit View Favorites Tools Help

Address http://pubs.usgs.gov/pinatubo/   Go   Links

FIRE and MUD
Eruptions and Lahars
of Mount Pinatubo, Philippines

Internet

▲ *A scene from the Mount Pinatubo volcanic eruption of 1991, in central Luzon.*

by the Spanish regime. She continues to be a source of inspiration to the people of the Philippines.

Fernando Amorsolo, born May 30, 1892, in Manila, earned a degree from the Lieco de Manila Art School in 1909. The father of fourteen children, Amorsolo became the Philippines' first national artist.

José Rizal was a renaissance man in the truest sense. A freedom fighter, writer, physician, and athlete, he is the national hero of the Philippines. He was executed in 1896 for his part in the Philippine rebellion against Spain. Today almost every town or plaza in the Philippines has a monument to him. His picture hangs on the wall in classrooms in schools and is also on the two-peso bill, the one-peso coin, and also on postage stamps.

Ferdinand Marcos, a Philippine political leader, was elected president of the Philippines in 1965. He established close ties with the United States, which supported him, but by 1973, Marcos had become a dictator. He was finally driven from power in 1986 by protests from opposition forces, even though he was declared the winner of the presidential election held that year. Marcos and his wife left the country. He died in exile in Hawaii in 1989. Marcos's wife, Imelda, became just as well known as he was, but for a different reason. Her extravagance was criticized, especially since millions of Filipinos were living in poverty while her husband was in power. After her husband's death, Mrs. Marcos was allowed to return to the Philippines.

Corazon Aquino, continuing in the tradition of Gabriela Silang, took her husband's place in Philippine politics after he was assassinated. Benigno Aquino, who had led a movement to oust President Marcos, was killed in 1983 after returning to the Philippines from exile in the United States. When the government agents accused of his murder were found not guilty, Mrs. Aquino decided to run for the presidency against Marcos. Both sides claimed victory in the 1986 election, and Marcos was declared the winner, but many people believed the election results had been tampered with. To protest the results, Mrs. Aquino organized strikes and boycotts and received the support of the powerful Roman Catholic Church in the Philippines as well as that of key members of the military. Thousands of Filipinos took to the streets in demonstrations against Marcos, who had no choice but to leave the country. Mrs. Aquino's presidency, the first by a woman in her country, was notable in restoring democracy to the Philippines.

Chapter 2

Land and Climate

The Philippines covers a total land area of 115,830 square miles. That is an area a little larger than Arizona. Many of the islands or islets that make up this country have less than a square mile of total land area. Only about two fifths of the islands have names. The islands of the Philippines are bordered by five bodies of water: the Philippine Sea, the Luzon Strait, the Sulu Sea, the South China Sea, and the Celebes Sea.

At one time, most of the country was covered with thick, lush forests. In the 1950s, lumber companies began to destroy much of the forest, and today only about one tenth of the land area is still forest.

▶ Main Island Groups

Narrow coastal plains, rich inland valleys, rolling hills, and high mountains can all be found in the Philippines. Major lowland plains are the Central Plain and Cagayan Valley on Luzon, and the Agusan Valley and Cotabato Valley on Mindanao. Mountain ranges include the Cordillera and Sierra Madre on Luzon.

Three main groups of islands make up the Philippines: the Luzon group (Luzon, Mindoro, and Palawan); the Visayan group (Bohol, Cebu, Leyte, Masbate, Negros, Panay, and Samar); and the third group is the island of Mindanao.

▶ The Ring of Fire

The Philippines is a beautiful country, yet it is prone to more natural disasters than any place on earth. One reason is because it is located in an area of the world called "the ring of fire," known for frequent earthquakes and volcanic eruptions. Earthquakes, mud slides, floods, volcanic eruptions, and typhoons (tropical hurricanes) are all common on the islands. From 1975 to 2000,

▲ A map of the Philippines.

there were two hundred fifty natural disasters in the Philippines, which caused 37,000 deaths.[1]

There are more than two hundred twenty volcanoes in the Philippines. Twenty-three of these are considered active. Mount Apo in Mindanao is the country's highest mountain at 9,692 feet above sea level. Mount Pulog in Luzon is the second highest mountain, at 9,613 feet.

River systems in the Philippines include the Pulangi, which flows into the Mindanao River; the Agusan, in Mindanao, which flows north into the Mindanao Sea; the Cagayan in northern Luzon; and the Pampanga, which flows south from Central Luzon into Manila Bay. Laguna de Bay, southeast of Manila Bay, is the largest freshwater lake in the Philippines. One of the deepest spots in all the oceans is off the northeastern coast of Mindanao. It is called the Philippine Trench and is 34,578 feet below the surface of the Pacific Ocean.

Two Seasons

The Philippines has a tropical climate, which means it is usually hot and humid year-round. The average annual temperature is 90°F. There are only two seasons: a dry season from March to May and a wet season from June to October. During the wet season, monsoon rains and typhoons are common.

Unique Plants and Animals

The Philippines is one of the most biologically diverse countries in the world. A wide variety of vegetation grows there, including banyan and palm trees and thick groves of bamboo. The islands have more than ten thousand species of flowering plants and ferns and over three thousand species of trees. More species of trees grow on the

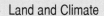
slopes of a single volcano, such as Banahaw, where jungle still exists, than in the entire United States.[2]

Wild animals, including deer, wild hogs, monkeys, and a small buffalo called the tamaraw, are also found in the Philippines. There are at least 739 known species of birds and more than 2,000 varieties of fish, including sardines, mackerel, tuna, milkfish, and sea bass. The carabao, a type of water buffalo, is the main domestic animal in the Philippines. Farmers use the carabao to pull plows and other heavy loads.

The Philippines is also home to 510 species of mammals, birds, frogs, and lizards that are found nowhere else

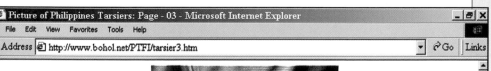

Picture of Philippines Tarsiers: Page - 03 - Microsoft Internet Explorer

File   Edit   View   Favorites   Tools   Help

Address http://www.bohol.net/PTFI/tarsier3.htm   Go   Links

The Tarsier can rotate its head almost all the way around and has adhesive pads on its limbs that allow it to cling to branches vertically or horizontally.

PREVIOUS Picture = NEXT Picture

Internet

The Philippine tarsier, one of the world's rarest animals, is named for the long tarsal bones that form its ankles. These bones allow the tarsier to leap as much as ten feet from tree to tree.

on earth. One of the smallest and rarest animals in the world that is found only in the Philippines is the Philippine tarsier. This little mammal, which has huge, owl-like eyes, has often been called "the smallest monkey in the world," but it is not a monkey.[3] It is a primate, more closely related to lemurs, lorises, and bush babies than to monkeys and apes. The Philippine tarsier is found only in the southern Philippine islands of Bohol, Samar, Leyte, and Mindanao. The population of this threatened species is rapidly declining as more and more of its forest habitats are destroyed. Environmentalists are trying to save the Philippine tarsier before this unique little creature becomes extinct.

The Chocolate Hills

One of the most unusual landforms in the Philippines is a group of egg-shaped hills on Bohol Island. They have a parched, brown color during the dry season. This is probably why they are called the Chocolate Hills. There are many legends that explain how these odd-looking mounds were formed, but the Chocolate Hills were most likely once limestone deposits under the sea that were lifted by the earth's plates and then smoothed out by erosion.

Culture

Scientists are not really sure how the first people came to the Philippines, but it is thought that they may have come over from the Asian mainland on a land bridge that existed then. Today, most Filipinos are related ethnically to Malaysians and Indonesians.

There are 84.5 million people living in the Philippines, with more than one hundred cultural minority groups. Filipino or Pilipino, which developed from Tagalog, is the national language. Many people also speak English, and it is the language used in secondary schools across the country.

Education is seen as very important in the Philippines, even though many people there never go to college. Still, the literacy rate is rather high. About 90 percent of Philippine adults can read and write. By law, children from seven to twelve years of age must attend school through at least the sixth grade.

▶ Where East Meets West

The Philippines is often described as being where East meets West, since the country is a mix of both Western and Eastern traditions and cultures.

The Filipinos often take something from either the West or the East and make it uniquely their own. Jeepneys are a good example of this. The Japanese controlled the Philippines for much of World War II, but the United States was in control of Manila by early 1945, leaving

▲ A Filipino boy sips coconut milk.

behind many U.S. Army Jeeps. Filipinos decided to change these Jeeps to fit their needs and culture. Known as jeepneys, the vehicles can often fit as many as fifteen people. They follow a set route and stop wherever the traveler needs to. They are a cheap form of transportation that is uniquely Filipino.

▶ The Family

The family is very important in Philippine culture. In rural areas, children are born at home, and they are cared for by their mother, father, older brothers and sisters, grandparents, aunts, and uncles. Children are taught that they must consider everyone in the family in everything that they do. Respect for elders is important, and most Filipinos are expected to care for their elderly parents.

▶ Religion

Long ago, before so many outside influences, the people of the islands worshiped the spirits of nature and the spirits of their ancestors, which they felt guarded the earth. Later, as foreign traders came to the islands, they brought their religions with them. Some of these early traders were from China, others were from Arab countries, so Buddhism and Islam made their way to the islands. When Spanish explorers came to the Philippines in the sixteenth century, they brought Christianity in the form of Roman Catholicism. The islands' first royal governor, Miguel López de Legazpi, tried to convert everyone in the islands to Christianity. But many of the people in the southern islands remained Muslim.

Today, the Philippines is the only predominantly Christian nation in Asia. About 85 percent of Filipinos are Roman Catholics, and many other Filipinos belong to other Christian denominations. About 5 percent of the population is Muslim. A small percent of the population is Buddhist. Some Filipinos believe, as their ancestors did, in animism by worshipping the spirits of the plant and animal world.

▶ Sports

Although American sports such as baseball and basketball are popular in the Philippines, traditional sports including *arnis* and *sipa* are also popular. Arnis resembles fencing but is done with wooden sticks. Sipa is a lot like volleyball except that players use their feet, instead of their hands and arms, to hit the ball.

One sport that is uniquely Philippine is *sabong*, or cockfighting. Most towns have an area called a *sabungan*

▲ This church in Las Piñas, on the island of Luzon, features an organ whose pipes are made of bamboo.

or *galleria*, which is most often a round structure with a roofed pit and bleachers that surround it. Inside, rooster fights take place. A man called the *kristo* or *casador* moves around the arena, taking bets as to which bird will win. The *sentenciador* announces the winner of this bloody sport. If one of the birds is killed in the fight, his owner takes him home and cooks him in a special dish called *talunan*, which means "loser's repast."[1]

Fiestas

Fiestas, which were brought to the Philippines by Spain, are an important part of Philippine culture. There are almost a hundred different fiestas in the Philippines every year. A fiesta is like a big party, even though most fiestas have a religious theme. Every town or barrio has its own patron saint. Each year the people have a fiesta to honor them, including the Ati-Atihan Festival in Kalibo, Aklan; the Moriones Festival celebrated on a few islands; and the Water Festival in San Juan. During fiesta time, the entire town celebrates with special food and parades, beauty pageants, and group contests. In the evenings, there are dances and partying in the streets.

Dance

Traditional and modern dance are part of Filipino culture. The *tinikling* is the national folk dance of the Philippines. For this dance, two boys and two girls hop between bamboo poles that other people hold just above the ground. The poles are struck together in time to music or people clapping, so the boys and girls have to be careful and hop between the poles at the right time, or they will be caught by the bamboo. This dance was created to imitate the movement of tikling birds as they gracefully dodged bamboo traps set by rice farmers.

The *singkil* is another version of this dance. It involves four bamboo poles and large paper fans. Singkil is said to be a dance of Muslim royalty. According to a Filipino legend, this dance developed when a fairy or nymph played a joke on a princess as she walked through the woods. The fairy created an earthquake that made the trees shake and rocks roll against each other. The fairy wanted to make it difficult for the princess to walk through the woods, but

Aklan, the oldest province in the Philippines, is home to many colorful festivals, including the one pictured above.

the princess continued to skip through the forest no matter what happened around her.

Music

Since A.D. 300, gong music has been played throughout the archipelago and is still performed in the northern and southern Philippines in musical forms known as *gangsa* and *kulitang*. A traditional Filipino song is the *kundiman*, a classic love song. Historically, this type of song was usually sung by a young man to express his unworthiness of a girl's love. The music of the Philippines has also been influenced by China, Japan, India, and Arabia.

Economy

In A.D. 982, China was the first country to trade with the Philippines. By around 1100, traders from India, Borneo, Sumatra, Java, Siam (Thailand), and Japan made the islands part of their trade routes, too. Trade was friendly with China, probably because during the fourteenth and fifteenth centuries, tribal leaders of the Philippines made regular visits to Beijing to honor the Chinese emperor.[1]

▶ The Economy Under Spanish Rule

Friendly trade with other countries continued until the arrival of the Spanish, with Ferdinand Magellan, in 1521. Magellan, a Portuguese navigator who sailed for Spain, led an expedition to find an alternate spice route to the west. When Magellan landed in the Philippines during that expedition, he claimed the islands for Spain. Not long after that, the islands became a Spanish colony.

The economy changed greatly under Spanish rule. The Spanish introduced forced labor and heavy taxes. Filipinos, who had been used to bartering, were made to pay one fifth of every gold nugget they had to Spain.[2] Some Filipino landowners and merchants were able to become rich under Spanish rule, but most Filipinos became poorer than ever.

▶ Today's Agriculture and Industry

Throughout history, the economy of the Philippines has depended mainly on agricultural products and lumber.

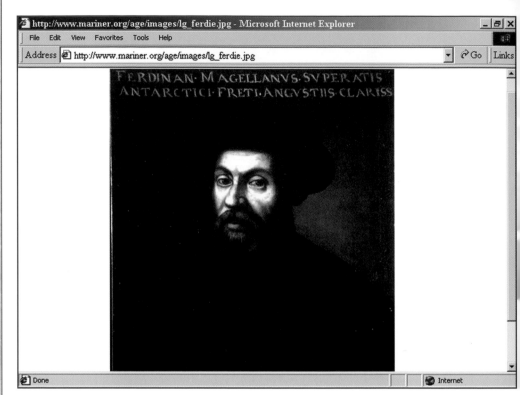

http://www.mariner.org/age/images/lg_ferdie.jpg - Microsoft Internet Explorer

File   Edit   View   Favorites   Tools   Help

Address http://www.mariner.org/age/images/lg_ferdie.jpg   Go   Links

FERDINAN·MAGELLANVS·SVPERATIS
ANTARCTICI·FRETI·ANGVSTIIS·CLARISS

Done   Internet

▲ *Ferdinand Magellan, sailing for Spain, was the first European explorer to reach the Philippines.*

Although those two areas are still important, manufacturing now surpasses all other industries in product value, and there are more factories in the Philippines than ever before. The country produces everything from cement to cigarettes. The largest percentage of manufactured goods are food, textiles, and tobacco products.

Rice is the country's major food crop. Corn, sweet potatoes, bananas, coconuts, mangoes, pineapples, and sugarcane are also grown there. These crops are used by Filipinos themselves and are also exported to other countries. Filipinos also raise water buffalo, cattle, chickens, goats, horses, and hogs on farms.

The Philippines also has many mineral and metallic resources. Gold, silver, copper, nickel, chromium, lead, and even salt are mined in the islands. Coal is mined and used as an alternative to petroleum imports, which are much more costly. Unfortunately, mining has brought with it serious problems from pollution.

▷ Dwindling Natural Resources and Other Problems

At one time, hardwood trees were one of the country's most valuable resources. But years of unregulated lumbering have destroyed much of the forestland. However, woody plants such as bamboo and rattan are still plentiful and are used to make furniture and baskets.

Fishing is still an important industry in the Philippines. There are many fishermen who operate small boats in the coastal waters of the islands. Crabs, shrimp, oysters, sardines, anchovies, tuna, scad, and mackerel are found in these waters. Fish makes up a good portion of the Philippine diet, so much of what is caught is sold within the islands. The fishing industry has suffered, however, because coastal and inland waters have become polluted in some areas, and overfishing has lowered fish populations.

In addition to pollution and decreasing natural resources, the Philippines faces serious economic problems, many which can be traced back to the practices of the Marcos administration more than twenty years ago. The Asian financial crisis of 1997 also affected the country, although the Philippines fared better than many other Asian countries. Severe weather conditions, including prolonged droughts and the eruption of Mount Pinatubo, have hurt agricultural exports. Political crises within the government of the

▲ *This early-twentieth-century photograph shows some proud lumberers in a region of Mindoro. Unfortunately, many of the forests that once dominated the landscape of the islands have vanished because of unregulated lumbering.*

Philippines and foreign influences have combined to slow the country's economic growth. There is hope, as the Philippine government has made some strides in economic reform, but the country is still billions of dollars in debt to foreign banks.

History

The Aeta, a small, dark-skinned people from Borneo, Sumatra, and Malaya, were most likely the first people to inhabit the Philippines. They were hunter-gatherers and skilled in jungle survival. Fossil remains show that the Aeta probably came to the islands 30,000 years ago by way of a land bridge. (Descendants of the Aeta still live in the Philippines.) Later migrations came by water, taking place over thousands of years. Malays from Indonesia and Malaysia settled along the coasts of the Philippines around 3,000 B.C.

The people in these widely scattered islands came to be organized socially and politically into a basic settlement unit known as a barangay. Barangays were communities of between fifty and one hundred families. The chief of each barangay was known as a datu.

Islam became established in the Sulu Archipelago and then in Mindanao by the early 1500s. It reached Manila by 1565. The Muslims introduced the idea of territorial states, and the rulers of such states had power over the datu.

▶ The Arrival of the Spanish

In 1521, the first Spanish expedition, which was led by the Portuguese navigator Ferdinand Magellan, landed on the island of Cebu in the Philippines. Magellan, on a voyage around the world, claimed the islands for Spain. He befriended some inhabitants of the islands, but not all.

The Mactan chieftain Lapu Lapu refused to pay tribute to the Spanish. When Magellan and some of his soldiers traveled to Mactan Island on April 27, 1521, to punish Lapu Lapu, the chieftain and his men killed the explorer. Datu Lapu Lapu is considered by Filipinos to be their country's first hero.

For the next forty years, more Spanish explorers sailed to the Philippines. The first permanent Spanish settlement was established in 1565 when Miguel López de Legazpi, the Philippines' first royal governor, arrived in Cebu from New Spain (present-day Mexico). The islands had earlier been named after Prince Philip of Spain. When Philip became king, he made the islands a Spanish colony.

The Philippines remained a colony of Spain for over three hundred years. Under Spanish colonial rule, most Filipinos were tenant farmers, laborers, or servants. They were made to follow Spanish customs. Many Filipinos were unhappy with life under Spanish rule and staged revolts for independence. One notable fight against the Spanish in the 1760s was led by a woman, Gabriela Silang. She died a martyr for her people.

In the 1800s, the Philippines became a wealthy nation due to foreign trade, and children of wealthy Filipinos began attending universities in Manila and in Europe. When they returned home, some of those young adults became involved in movements to free the Philippines from Spanish rule. One of them, José Rizal, a physician, scholar, and writer, became a leader in the freedom movement. He worked for reform until 1896, when the Spanish authorities executed him for his actions. Many other Filipinos did not want to remain under Spain's rule, and they continued the fight for their independence.

▲ *Emilio Aguinaldo led the Philippines in its war against the American occupation. Here, Aguinaldo, front row, third from the right, is joined by other Filipino revolutionaries.*

▶ The Fight Against Colonial Rule

In 1892, an office clerk named Andres Bonifacio formed a secret revolutionary society called the *Katipunan* and tried to overthrow the Spanish government. Bonifacio was killed during the revolt, however, and Emilio Aguinaldo, a local chief of the Katipunan, became the new leader of the revolutionary forces. The Spanish government, which wanted the revolt to end, promised political reform if Aguinaldo would leave the country and stop the revolt. Aguinaldo agreed, and left the country for Hong Kong. But at the time, the Filipinos were not the only ones angry with Spain.

The Spanish-American War

In April 1898, after the sinking of the USS *Maine* in Havana, Cuba's harbor, the United States declared war on Spain, which it believed had sunk the ship. On May 1, the U.S. fleet destroyed the Spanish fleet in Manila Bay, which marked the first major battle of the war. Two weeks later, Aguinaldo returned to the Philippines and formed an army to fight along with the Americans, and together they defeated the Spanish forces in the islands. On June 12, Aguinaldo declared the Philippines to be independent, although fighting continued until August. This independence did not last long, however. In December 1898, the United States and Spain signed a treaty ending the war. In the treaty, Spain ceded the Philippines to the United States for $20 million.

▲ *This painting captures the U.S. fleet in action against the Spanish fleet during the Battle of Manila, in the Spanish-American War.*

The War Against American Occupation

Aguinaldo and others who had fought with the Americans against Spain were angered by the terms of the treaty. Aguinaldo accused the United States of breaking its promise to make the Philippines independent. He and his army began fighting the Americans on February 4, 1899. By March 1901, the Americans had captured Aguinaldo and the fighting ended about a year later, with many Filipino lives lost. The Philippines remained an American colony, but tensions between Filipinos who wanted complete independence and the American colonial government continued.

World War II and Japanese Control

At first, the United States set up a colonial government in the Philippines with William Howard Taft serving as the first civilian governor. Later, in 1935, the United States let Filipinos hold government positions. That year, Filipinos elected their own president, Manuel L. Quezon.

The United States entered World War II in December 1941, after the Japanese attacked Pearl Harbor. Hours after that attack, the Japanese began bombing U.S. outposts in the Pacific, including in the Philippines. Within a few months, the Japanese controlled the islands. American and Filipino troops battled the Japanese for three years. Early in May 1942, some eighty thousand American and Filipino troops surrendered to the Japanese. They were forced to march seventy miles from the Bataan Peninsula to prison camps in Pampanga. Nearly ten thousand died of disease, starvation, or torture in what has become known as the Bataan Death March. What is not widely known is that for every American soldier who died on Bataan, twenty Filipinos perished. Finally, in 1945,

◀ *In 1935, Manuel Quezon became the first popularly elected president of the Philippines.*

the American and Filipino forces were able to defeat the Japanese and take back control of the Philippines.

▶ Independence at Last

On July 4, 1946, the United States granted full independence to the Philippines. Manuel Roxas became president, Manila became the capital (although Quezon City was the capital from 1948 to 1976), and the country adopted a constitution and system of government that were much like those of the United States.

The war had hurt the economy in the Philippines and damaged much of Manila. The newly independent nation was beset by many political problems and great poverty. A Communist-led group called *Hukbong Magpapalayang Bayan* (the People's Liberation Army) tried to take over the government. The Huks, as they were known, wanted to divide the property of wealthy landowners and give land to poor farmers. The Philippine army fought the Huks from 1949 until 1954, when they defeated them. The United States government had already provided the Philippines with economic aid, but the economy had not responded, so in 1950, more aid was sent to the islands. In return, the Philippine government let the United States set up an air force base and a naval base there. The economy of the Philippines began to improve. New factories were built, farmers began to use new, more modern methods to grow and harvest crops, yielding greater production, and trade with foreign countries increased.

The Marcos Years

In 1965, Ferdinand E. Marcos, a lawyer and aide to Manuel Roxas, ran for president of the Philippines. His slogans, "Let this nation be great again!" and "Forward the Filipino!," appealed to Filipinos, and he was elected.[1] Soon he helped create a new law that would improve the economy by encouraging foreign companies to build their factories in the islands. His administration had close ties to the United States. The economy did improve under Marcos, and he was elected to a second term.

Things did not go so smoothly for Marcos during his second term, however. He sent troops to fight the New People's Army, a group of Philippine Communists who tried to take over the government. The Philippine army was also involved in fighting the Moro National Liberation Front, a Muslim separatist group on Mindanao and several other southern islands.

In order to try to gain more control, President Marcos declared martial law in 1972. It gave the military the power to enforce the law. Marcos also had opposition leaders arrested. He postponed elections. He exercised absolute power over the country.

In 1980, opposition groups demanded an end to martial law. There were bombings in Manila. Marcos finally ended martial law in January 1981. In June, he was elected to a new six-year term even though many people were unhappy with his leadership.

Opposition to Marcos continued to increase. In 1983, his chief political opponent, Benigno Aquino, returned to the Philippines from exile and was assassinated. Aquino supporters accused the Philippine government of having a role in the assassination. Marcos appointed a commission to investigate the assassination, and their findings concluded that some members of the military had been involved, but a court in 1985 acquitted them.

▶ Corazon Aquino Becomes President

Political unrest and growing opposition led Marcos to hold another election in 1986. His opponent was Corazon Aquino, the widow of Benigno Aquino. The National Assembly declared Marcos the winner, but many believed election fraud had taken place. Aquino rallied opposition to Marcos in the form of protests and strikes, getting support from the Catholic Church and some members of the military. Ferdinand Marcos finally left office, and he and his wife were flown by an American military plane to Hawaii, where they lived in exile until Marcos's death in 1989.

Corazon Aquino was sworn in as president, promising to restore democracy to the Philippines and improve its economy. She was successful in bringing about democratic reforms, and in 1990 the earlier court decision that had acquitted members of the military in her husband's death was overturned. But she was less successful in improving the economy, which had suffered during the Marcos years. Aquino's administration was also threatened by Communist and other guerrilla groups who opposed the continuing influence of the United States. Aquino remained in office until 1992. That year, Fidel Ramos, her defense minister, was elected president.

▶ The 1990s and Beyond

Ramos was succeeded by Joseph Ejercito Estrada, an actor, who was elected president in 1998. He was removed from office and arrested in 2001 amid allegations of corruption.

Gloria Macapagal-Arroyo, Estrada's vice president, became the tenth president of the Philippines. An American expert on Asian affairs had this to say about President Macapagal-Arroyo: "In President Macapagal Arroyo the Philippine people have a leader who understands the burden of her office, the enormous demands on her leadership, and the necessity of defending the freedom of Filipinos Her victory was a victory for the rule of law and for Philippine democracy."[2]

▲ Former Philippine president Corazon Aquino, the first woman to serve her country as head of state, is pictured at a ceremony in Manila in August 2003 that marked the twentieth anniversary of her husband's death.

Chapter 6

Filipino Americans Today

Filipinos began arriving in the Americas in the sixteenth century, but not of their own accord. Spaniards began transporting Filipinos to their colonial holdings in the New World, where they put them to work as slaves. At least 4 million Filipinos were brought across the Pacific Ocean to the Americas aboard Spanish galleons, large square-rigged sailing ships. In the eighteenth century, many Filipinos started immigrating to America, looking for a better life. Filipinos in Acapulco crossed the Gulf of Mexico to Barataria Bay in Louisiana. They established seven fishing villages there. In the Battle of New Orleans, during the War of 1812, Filipinos fought for the United States against British forces.

▶ Immigration to the United States

The first large group of Filipinos to immigrate to America came after 1898, when the United States annexed the Philippines following the Spanish-American War. The largest emmigration from the Philippines to the United States was from 1906 to 1935. During that time, more than 125,000 Filipinos were brought to Hawaii to work on the sugarcane plantations. Filipinos also came to work on farms in California and in the canneries of Alaska. Their working and living conditions were difficult. And like many other immigrant groups who came to the United States, Filipinos, especially those who came during the years of the Depression, were not treated well by the citizens of their new homeland. They faced much of the same discrimination and restrictions that African Americans and other citizens of color did. Back then, Filipino Americans and other people of color could not eat in certain restaurants or meet or stay in certain hotels. They could use only certain restrooms and water fountains. They faced racial discrimination and were resented by some Americans who felt that Filipinos were taking jobs away from them.

Not all Filipino immigrants at the time were looking for work. Some were students who were sent to the United States to attend college. Later groups came because they served in the United States Navy. Both of those groups would go on to make important contributions to American life.

A third Filipino immigration began in 1945, with the end of World War II, and continued through 1965, since Filipinos who had served in the U.S. Armed Forces could become United States citizens. Filipinos had fought with the United States Army during the Second World War. In fact, the First and Second Filipino Regiments, who were segregated from other Army regiments, were among the most decorated combat units to serve in the Pacific theater of operations during the war.

The U.S. Immigration Act of 1965 was a turning point in Filipino immigration to the United States. As many as twenty thousand Filipinos, mostly doctors, nurses, and other professionals, began immigrating to the United States per year.

▶ Filipino Americans Today

Life in the United States has become better for Filipino Americans, although some discrimination does still exist.

Filipino Americans are among the most educated and accomplished in all fields and they earn among the highest incomes of immigrants in the United States.

According to the National Filipino Council, there are about 2.2 million Filipino Americans today.[1] This makes Filipinos the fastest-growing and second-largest Asian population in America, after the Chinese. Of all immigrants, Filipinos are second only to Mexicans in rates of immigration and numbers of immigrants. And with more jobs available to women, there are now more female Filipino Americans than male Filipino Americans. Filipino Americans have settled in all parts of the United States.

▶ Filipino Culture in the United States

After the Philippines was ceded to the United States in 1898, American soldiers and other Americans served as teachers in Philippine schools. English became the language used in public and private schools in the islands. Now Filipino, as well as English, is taught in the primary grades. American textbooks were also used, so Filipino students were taught American history, literature, and culture. As a result, only one percent of the Filipino-American population cannot speak English at all.

It is important to Filipino Americans to preserve their culture by observing the customs and traditions of their homeland. Philippine food, dance, newspapers, clothes, art, and other elements of Philippine culture are available in the United States today. Filipino Americans have also formed regional associations in which they meet with other Filipinos who emigrated from the same region that they did. A movement toward instituting Filipino American studies in school and college curricula is also under way.

Publications, Food, and Dance

There are many newspapers and magazines printed in the United States especially for Filipino Americans. The *Philippine News* (in California) and the *Filipino Reporter* (from New York City) are two of the most popular newspapers. *Filipinas* and *The Special Edition Press: The Filipino American Quarterly* are two popular magazines written for Filipino Americans. Los Angeles, California, which has a large Filipino-American population, also broadcasts radio and television programs geared toward Filipino Americans.

Filipino Americans have introduced traditional Filipino foods such as *pansit* (rice noodles) and *lumpia*

The LIKHA Pilipino Folk Ensemble, based in California, was founded in 1992 to preserve and present Philippine culture in its many forms.

(egg rolls) to American culture. These foods are enjoyed at parties, festivals, and in restaurants.

In the arts, Filipino-American dance and cultural groups perform throughout the country as well as abroad. One of the most well known is the Folklorico Filipino Dance Company of New York. This company has over fifty members who take part in New York parades, cultural festivals, and other presentations each year. Another cultural group, the LIKHA Pilipino Folk Ensemble, based in the San Francisco Bay Area, was created in 1992 to preserve and promote Philippine culture and tradition not only in dance but also in music, literature, crafts, costume, and art. *LIKHA* is a Pilipino term meaning "creation." The ensemble has toured other U.S. cities as well as cities in Europe and Asia.

▶ Famous Filipino Americans

Filipino Americans have distinguished themselves in many fields. Roman Gabriel was a well-known quarterback for the Los Angeles Rams. Named the league's Most Valuable Player in 1969, he spent sixteen years in the NFL and was four times voted All Pro.

Victoria Manalo, born in San Francisco of an English mother and Filipino father, was the first woman to win Olympic gold medals in both platform and springboard diving. She accomplished this in the 1948 Olympics, held in London, England.

Filipino Americans Alex Tizon and Byron Acohido, journalists with the *Seattle Times*, were awarded the Pulitzer Prize in journalism on May 29, 1997, for investigative and beat reporting.

Lou Diamond Phillips, Rob Schneider, Nia Peeples, and Tia Carrere are all actors of Filipino heritage.

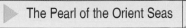

Pista Review - Microsoft Internet Explorer

File   Edit   View   Favorites   Tools   Help

Address ⬚ http://1grid.net/pistaorg/programguide/pulitzer.htm ▼ 𝒞 Go   Links

Byron Acohido & Alex Tizon

 Printed in the 1997 Pista Review

Alex Tizon (l-r) and Byron Acohido inside the Seattle Times newsroom learn they are both Pulitzer Prize winners. The announcement was made by President George Rupp of Columbia University on April 7, 1997.

Pista sa Nayon is a Seafair event

Feature Articles
Program Guide

Good things come to those who write. Winning a Pulitzer Prize, however, is not just a good thing. It's a most prestigious and once-in-a-lifetime experience. A Pulitzer, if not the highest, is one of the highest journalism award; the prizes have been awarded by the Columbia University since 1917 after Joseph Pulitzer, an American newspaper publisher. On April 7, 1997, two Filipino

⬚ Internet

▲ *Filipino Americans Alex Tizon and Byron Acohido, reporters for the* Seattle Times, *were awarded the highest prize in journalism when each won a Pulitzer Prize in 1997.*

Many other Filipino Americans have contributed greatly to the life and culture of the United States without gaining as much fame. A Filipino was one of the founders of the city of Los Angeles, and descendants of the Aeta in Olonggapo taught U.S. military forces jungle-survival skills that were used during the Vietnam War. Filipino Americans have overcome much hardship, including racial discrimination, to become a vital part of the American tapestry, and their athletic, cultural, and scientific contributions are a testament to a proud heritage that values education.

The Philippines Facts

1. Borgna Brunner, ed., *Time Almanac 2003* (Boston: Information Please, 2002), p. 839.

2. Ibid.

Chapter 1. The Pearl of the Orient Seas

1. Alfredo and Grace Roces, *Culture Shock! Philippines* (Portland, Oreg.: Graphic Arts Center Publishing Company, 2000), p. 154.

2. Ibid., p. 35.

Chapter 2. Land and Climate

1. "Eye on the Philippines," n.d.,<http://www.globaleye .org.uk/ secondary_autumn2001/eyeon/land.html> (May 31, 2003).

2. Albrecht G. Schaefer, Wolf Dietrich, Sylvia L. Mayuga, Roland Hanewald, *Explore the World, Nelles Guide, Philippines* (Munich: Nelles Verlag, 2000), p. 216.

3. Meet the Philippines, "Save the Philippine Tarsier," n.d., <http://www.philippinetarsier.org/meet/meet_faqs.htm> (May 31, 2003).

Chapter 3. Culture

1. Alfredo and Grace Roces, *Culture Shock! Philippines* (Portland, Oreg.: Graphic Arts Center Publishing Company, 2000), p. 79.

Chapter 4. Economy

1. Russ Kerr, Joe Bindloss, Virginia Jealous, Caroline Liou, Mic Looby, *Philippines* (Melbourne, Oakland, London, Paris: Lonely Planet Publications, 2000), p. 17.

2. Ibid., p. 36.

Chapter 5. History

1. James Hamilton-Paterson, *America's Boy: A Century of Colonialism in the Philippines* (New York: Henry Holt and Company, 1998), p. 196.

2. Hearing before the Subcommittee on East Asian and Pacific Affairs of the Committee on Foreign Relations, United States Senate, One Hundred Seventh Congress, First Session, March 6, 2001. "The Philippines: Present Political Status and Its Role in the New Asia," p. 32.

Chapter 6. Filipino-Americans Today

1. Philippines News Central.com, "The Filipino Americans, Yesterday and Today," n.d., <Veltisezar Bautista, http://www .philnewscentral.com/cgi-bin/redirect.cgi?url=yes_today.html> (May 31, 2003).

Further Reading

Gordon, Sharon. *Philippines*. Salt Lake City: Benchmark Books, 2003.

Gray, Shirley Wimblish. *The Philippines*. Danbury, Conn.: Children's Press, 2003.

Green, Carl R. *The Spanish-American War*. Berkeley Heights, N.J.: Enslow Publishers, Inc., 2002.

Italia, Bob. *Philippines*. Edina, Minn.: ABDO Publishing, 2002.

Kinkade, Sheila. *Children of the Philippines*. Minneapolis: Carolrhoda Books, 1996.

Lepthien, Emilie U. *The Philippines*. Danbury, Conn.: Children's Press, 2000.

Nickles, Greg. *Philippines: The People*. New York: Crabtree Publishers, 2002.

Schraff, Anne E. *A Ticket to the Philippines*. Minneapolis: Carolrhoda Books, 2000.

Wee, Jessie. *Philippines*. Broomall, Penn.: Chelsea House Publishing, 1998.

A

Aguinaldo, Emilio, 33, 34, 35
Amorsolo, Fernando, 14
Apo, Mount, 18
Aquino, Benigno, 15, 38
Aquino, Corazon, 15, 38, 39

B

Banaue rice terraces, 12
barrios, 10
Bataan Death March, 35
Bonifacio, Andres, 33

C

Chocolate Hills, 20
climate, 18
culture, 21–26

E

economy, 27–30, 37, 38
Estrada, Joseph Ejercito, 39

F

fiestas, 25

G

Gabriel, Roman, 44
geography, 10, 16–18

H

history, 11, 13–15, 21–22, 29–30,
    31–39
Hukbong Magpapalayang Bayan, 36

I

Islam, 31

J

jeepneys, 21, 22

K

Katipunan, 33

L

Lapu Lapu, 31, 32
LIKHA Pilipino Folk Ensemble,
    43, 44
López de Legazpi, Miguel, 23, 32

M

Macapagal-Arroyo, Gloria 39
Magellan, Ferdinand, 27, 28, 31, 32
Manalo, Victoria, 44
Manila, 12, 13, 14, 36, 37
Marcos, Ferdinand, 15, 37, 38
Marcos, Imelda, 15
Muslims, 23, 31

P

Philippine Trench, 18
Pilipino, 21
Pinatubo, Mount, 13, 14, 29
Pulog, Mount, 18

Q

Quezon, Manuel L., 35, 36
Quezon City, 13, 36

R

Ramos, Fidel, 38, 39
religion, 15, 23
Ring of fire, 17
Rizal, José, 14, 32
Roxas, Manuel, 36, 37

S

Sabong, 23
Silang, Maria Josefa Gabriela, 13,
    15, 32
singkil, 25
sipa, 23
Spanish-American War, 34, 40

T

Taft, William Howard, 35
Tagalog, 21
Talunan, 24
tarsier, 19
tinikling, 25

U

U.S. Immigration Act of 1965, 41
USS *Maine*, 34